The Great Escape

Ron Marr

For more information and for other resources, contact:
ChristLife, Inc.
1642 Michigan Ave.
Niagara Falls, NY 14305
716-284-7625
Fax: 716-285-5409
E-Mail: pastormarr@adelphia.net
            christlife@adelphia.net
Web Sites: www.pastormarr.com
            www.christpassion.net

Italicized Scripture references are based on the King James Version transposed into modern English.

Library of Congress Cataloging-in-Publication Data

Marr, Ron
        The Great Escape/Ron Marr
            p.   cm.
    ISBN: 0-9758993-1-7   (pbk.)
    1. Christian Gospel   2. Salvation 3. Heaven—the way to   I. Marr, Ron   II. Title

We acknowledge a debt of love to the many who have directly or indirectly contributed to this book. Among these are tract distributors, and Walter Bleecker and Florence Biros.

Contents

This wee book is written especially for caring people to give to people they care about.

We trust that you'll be glad a million years from now that you used it well.

Remember we're all imperfect people in an imperfect world. That's why we need heaven! If anything I say, um, or do offends or grieves, please forgive me, and accept my apology and my imperfection.

Part One—
It's a Life or Death Matter

Now, I may be wrong,

But chances are

you're in big trouble
with God!

Yes, He's the God of Love.

Incredible as it seems,
He loves you so much
He sent His Son to die
the most awful death
for you.

He loves you and wants
always to help you and do
for you the very best He can.
God is Love (1 John 4:16).

But, we all start out in bad
trouble with Him.
You and I—all of us.

God Himself tells us,
*All have sinned and come
short of the glory of God*
(His standard of perfection)

(Romans 3:23)

And the wages of sin is death

(Romans 6:23).

Now, that's really big trouble.

And it's certainly
not something
you want to hear.

Nor is it something
I like telling you.

Nor is it something
God planned
or takes delight in.

Never.

It's just the way it is.
Inescapably,
sin is the root,
death the fruit.

Oh, I wish with all my heart
that I could honestly tell
you it isn't so,
that we're not
under a death sentence.

But regardless of what
I might want
—or you may want—
the Bible truth is
that no matter how *good*
or *bad* you may be,
all have sinned,
and that includes you and me.

The wages of sin *is* death.
And this death isn't
just physical death,
the last breath,
the last heartbeat.

The great God of love Himself says of the end of time as we know it now, *Death and hell are cast into the lake of fire. This is the second death. And whoever was not found written in the book of life was cast into the lake of fire*

(Revelation 20:14,15).

He continues the description
of this awful destiny
that awaits all who persist
undeterred in their own ways:

*The Son of man shall send
forth his angels, and they
shall gather out of his
kingdom . . . them that do
iniquity and shall cast them
into a furnace of fire:
there shall be wailing and
gnashing of teeth*
(Matthew 13:41,42).

*And these shall go away
into everlasting punishment:
but the righteous
into life eternal*

(Matthew 25:46).

Read this any way you want,
it's still a picture of terrible
suffering that no sane person
could ever want to endure.
I cringe at the thought.
The very idea pains me.
I want to run away from it.
I don't want to face it.

See page 98.

I'm sure you don't either.
So, go ahead.
Get mad at me if you want.

You don't have to
put up with this!
Besides, I must be wrong.

A good God of love couldn't
possibly consign anyone
to an eternal hell!
Could He?

No!
He couldn't, and
He won't.

It isn't God
who sends any human
to hell.
It's man himself
and his own sin.

Any person goes to hell not by
God's choice, but by his own.
God warns mankind of the
danger of hell,
and provides the most
wonderful way of escape.

What will you do about it?

Of course, you can throw
this book away,
play ostrich,
put your head in the sand
so you don't see the terrible
threat that may be about
to gobble you up—
or the marvelous way
of escape God has provided.

But,
suppose there's a chance,
just a chance,
that God knows
something you don't.

Just suppose that a horrible hell
—whatever its exact nature—
awaits those who won't take
His way out.

Do you really want
to risk everything
on the chance
that God may be wrong?

Wouldn't you really rather
take His word on it . . .
and His way out?
If you take His word on it,
and His way of escape,
you have nothing to lose
and everything to gain.
If you refuse, you have
everything to lose,
nothing to gain.

Now, get this!
Everything hangs
on what follows!
Don't miss it.

When God gave us
the bad news,
"The wages of sin is death,"
in the same breath
He also gave us
wonderful good news,
*"BUT, the gift of God
is eternal life
through Jesus Christ
our Lord"*

(Romans 6:23).

God,
in all His love,
designed a way
through the sacrificial death
and miraculous resurrection
of Christ Jesus
to give you and me,
not the eternal death
we deserve,
but the eternal life
we do not deserve.

And that eternal life
we know as

HEAVEN

. . . with all that word
conveys

—Perfection in
Every Direction

—Nothing Good
Ever Denied You!

WOW!

I don't know anyone
so infinitely foolish as
to deliberately trade
this kind of heaven
in for that kind of hell,
do you?

But, if we do *nothing* to change the direction of our lives, that's exactly what we're doing—choosing hell in preference to heaven.

That's right!
All you have to do
is *nothing*.

So, what to do?

God Himself
has given you the answer.

God so loved the world that He gave His only begotten son that whoever believes in Him should not perish but have everlasting life

(John 3:16).

As many as received Him (Jesus), to them gave He power to become the sons of God, even to them that believe on His name

(John 1:12).

So, what to do?

*Do what millions of others
around the world
have done for
thousands of years.*

Believe that God sent Jesus
to be your sufficient Savior
to save you from all your sins
and their punishment.

Invite Him
to be your *Savior* and
Lord.

Pray something like this.
Mean it from your heart.
If you can't, read it again and
again until you can. But
whatever you do, don't put off
making this most important
of life's decisions—

Pray this
Prayer of Faith

Dear God,
I know I'm a sinner
in need of a Savior from my sin.
I've displeased and offended You.
I know that Jesus came to earth
from heaven to die for me
and be a sufficient sacrifice
for my sin.
I turn from my sin to receive Him
as my Savior and Lord.
I believe that right now
You forgive all my sins
and I'm Your child by faith,
on my way to heaven.
I know that
no good deeds I've done
have contributed anything
toward my eternal salvation.
I'm saved by God's mercy alone.
I can't thank You enough
for the awful sacrifice Jesus made
as He suffered and died for me,
but I do thank You
and give You praise.
And I'll seek to love You,
please You, and serve You.
I'll seek to walk with You
and learn from You,
Your Word, and Your people
all the rest of my life here.
I pray this in Jesus' name. AMEN.

Now, if you're not sure you
meant this Prayer of Faith
from your heart, . . . if you're
not sure you've received
Christ as
your Savior and Lord, . . .
read this Prayer of Faith
again, and, if necessary,
again and again until you do
mean it and
you actually do receive Him as
your Savior and Lord.

If you have questions, you may find the answers as you read on. Also, you should go to web site www.pastormarr.com.

Or e-mail us at pastormarr@adelphia.net.

Be sure to give us your phone number and e-mail and postal addresses so we can respond appropriately. We'll try to get you the help you need. Find a Bible and read the Gospel of John, especially Chapter 3. Read it until its meaning is clear. Turn to page 121 for help.

From time to time read
this Prayer of Faith
to remind you of what you
have done
in receiving Christ
as your Savior and Lord.
Or, if you haven't yet
received Him,
read it to help you
receive Him
at the earliest
possible moment.
The main thing right now is
not to neglect the well being
of your soul any longer.
It's far too dangerous
a thing to do.
Stick with it until you're sure
your sins have been forgiven
and you're on
your way to heaven.
Keep right on reading
this book.
Ask God in simple trust
to give you the help you need.

If you've prayed the Prayer of Faith sincerely, but you're just not sure of your salvation, turn to page 123.

Remember, whether you're 6 or 106, you're not sure you'll draw another breath. You're not sure whether in the next second you'll stand before God to answer for what you have done . . . especially whether you've taken this opportunity to receive Him as your Savior and Lord, to have your name written in the Book of Life, and to be sure you'll live perfectly happily with Him in heaven forever.

WHAT WILL IT BE?

Let me urge you,
if you still haven't prayed
the Prayer of Faith
with meaning, do it now.
It's on page 53.

NEXT

Once you have received Christ as your Savior and Lord and to get a good start on your walk with God:

•Read this Prayer of Faith daily to help confirm in your mind and spirit what you've done.

•Tell someone you've received Christ as your Savior and Lord, that with His help, you want to be different.

•Spend time reading your Bible and praying every day. If you don't have a Bible, go to a book store and get one.

•Talk with God as your loving Father. Talk to Him about everything. Trust Him for everything.

• Learn to fellowship with Him, trust, worship, praise and thank Him, listen to Him, and wait quietly on Him.

• Ask Him to confirm to you His voice . . . to teach you to listen and know Him.

• When you find yourself displeasing God, ask Him to forgive and cleanse you.

• Find a good Bible–believing church, and attend regularly. Make friends of others who have also received Jesus as their Savior.

• Help others find Christ as Savior and Lord. See page 121 for assistance in this.

Part Two—
Helpful
Thoughts

How Do I Know?

I have only one claim to authority for what I say. The Bible, the Holy Scriptures.

There's no book like it. It speaks authoritatively to every essential issue. When scientists said the earth was flat, the Bible spoke of the circle of the earth.

Without doubt, it gives us the highest code of morality and ethics in the ten commandments and their summary, *You shall love the Lord your God, with all your heart, and with all your soul, and with all your mind, and your neighbor as yourself* (Matthew 22:37-39).

The Bible records hundreds of prophecies that have been fulfilled. A great many of them predicted the coming of Christ Jesus to be our Savior hundreds of years in advance of its occurrence.

It has been proved to be wonderfully accurate.

I would not for a moment pin my hope for eternity elsewhere than on what it says. When it says, *There is no other name under heaven . . . whereby we must be saved*, I will do no less than put all my hope in that One, Christ Jesus my Lord and Savior (Acts 4:12).

If you have not yet put all your trust in Jesus Christ alone for your eternal salvation, if you have not yet received Him as your personal Savior and Lord, I pray you will today.

Turn back to page 53 and pray the Prayer of Faith in Jesus right now.

Not What You Know

Even should you know more than I do about all that I've written, it's not what you know that saves or condemns you. It's whether you've actually received Jesus Christ as your Lord and personal Savior—whether your hope for eternal salvation is in Him and no one and no thing else.

Where Are You Headed?

It would grieve me terribly to think that you might die, perhaps suddenly and unexpectedly, and go to hell. Our wonderful Lord Jesus suffered and died for you because He loved you so much He couldn't stand the thought of that happening to you.

He died for you so He could forgive your sin and care for you and share His love and fellowship with you now and eternally.

All you need to do is turn from your sin and receive Him as your Lord and Savior. If you haven't honestly done so yet, I ask you again to turn to page 53 and earnestly pray the Prayer of Faith that's there.

An Obligation of Love

Oh, my friend, I do hope my straightforwardness doesn't offend you.

You see, I've an obligation of love to lay my heart bare with you on this subject that is of the greatest importance to us both.

I really care for you. That's why I've prepared this book for you.

Also, Jesus Christ is very real to me, and I owe Him my love and loyalty. After all, He suffered in unbelievable agony, and died for me. And when I simply received Him and His free gift of eternal salvation, He forgave my sin, made me a child of God, and graciously, sweetly came to live within me and begin the transformation I so obviously need.

Oh, how I wish this process of transformation were much further along than it is!

I'm honestly sorry I'm not all you might expect. I really am.

But, bad as I may be, I genuinely do care for you.

And, if you still haven't received Jesus as your personal Savior, I pray you will right now, and then you'll be sure you're a child of God, your sins forgiven, and you're on your way to heaven.

I'm Just a Saved Sinner

I hope you haven't somehow got the idea that I think, because I'm His, I'm better than somebody else. I'm only a sinner saved by grace. I've done nothing, nor could I do anything, to deserve God's free gift of eternal salvation.

—Just admit I'm a sinner in need of a Savior—Just receive Him as my Savior and Lord.

Do You Need a Savior?

God in His holiness can receive into His family and His heaven only those who are morally perfect. But, the only human being who has ever met that standard is Jesus, Son of Man and Son of God.

Every other human, including you and me, has fallen short of that standard of perfection. We were born in sin, and we have sinned ever since. Only Jesus was born without sin and never sinned.

He taught and lived the highest standard of moral behavior.

For 2000 years He has lifted the defiled, the degraded, and the destructive, and elevated them to places of usefulness, hopefulness, and helpfulness.

When we come to Him for the forgiveness of our sin, receiving Him as our Savior and Lord, God places all His perfect righteousness to our account. And, right then, we are justified in the sight of God just as though we had never sinned.

We are born again into God's family, forgiven, and given eternal spiritual life and His perfect righteousness (John 3:16, Romans 4:5).

From there on we can come to Him freely for the forgiveness of each new sin as He brings it to our attention.

If we confess our sins, He is faithful and just to forgive us our sins, and to cleanse us from all unrighteousness (I John 1:9).

Then as we walk in fellowship with Him as our ongoing Savior, He covers all our unrecognized sin with the blood of His own sacrifice.

If we walk in the light as He is in the light, we have fellowship one with another, and the blood of Jesus Christ His son cleanses (keeps on cleansing) us from all sin (IJohn 1:7).

Don't Delay a Minute

I hope you've already received Christ as your Savior and Lord. If not, why not?

How can you give so much attention to things that last for such a short time?. . . Cars, houses, money, stocks and bonds, popularity, passing pleasures.

You can't take earthly possessions with you into eternity.

On the other hand, how can you give so little attention to things that last forever?. . . Your eternal salvation or condemnation.

Your soul's salvation from damnation in a horrible hell to eternal life in a marvelous heaven is the one thing that is really worthy of your attention.

—Until that is settled, nothing else really matters.

I would be the most unkind, uncaring, unfeeling person imaginable if I didn't make it my foremost work in life lovingly to tell you so.

Anyone who doesn't give their eternal destiny the foremost attention it demands must surely be the most foolish person imaginable.

Don't put it off. If you haven't yet, do it now.

Turn to page 53 and pray the Prayer of Faith.

God-Shaped Empty Spot

Someone has said, "There's a God-shaped empty spot in everyone." Pleasure cannot fill it. Popularity can't fill it. Profit and prosperity can't fill it. Not even health or happiness can fill it, as desirable as they may be. Nor yet can any degree of human peace, though it may top the list.

The Great Escape is from this and so very much more. This little book may be the most important book you ever read.

Mankind was made by God to live in harmony with Him, to enjoy fellowship with Him; and mankind can be satisfied with nothing less. Only God can fill that God-shaped empty spot that's in every one of us.

If you haven't yet received Jesus as your Savior and Lord, that empty spot is still there, and will be until you do. Turn to page 53. Pray the Prayer of Faith sincerely. Receive Him. He'll fill that empty spot with Himself.

Undeserved But Marvelous Mercy

It is by God's mercy alone that we are saved, as we simply trust Him. Even the faith we exercise in receiving Him and His salvation is the free gift of God. There is simply nothing we can do to earn our salvation. It is all of Him through His free grace and mercy, totally undeserved. So we have absolutely no grounds for pride or boasting. Left to our own devices we're not only without God but without hope.

By grace (God's mercy) are you saved through faith (by believing), and that not of yourselves. It is the gift of God, not of works, lest any man should boast (Ephesians 2:8,9).

Salvation is God's free gift bought for us by Jesus' death. Not a thing we do, no matter how good, can mean anything toward our salvation.

To the contrary, if we think we can somehow earn our salvation, all we're doing is adding to our sin and rebellion against God.

Our great sin is prideful Independence from God, and by trying somehow to earn our salvation instead of admitting there isn't a good thing in ourselves that God can value, we only demonstrate the justice of His judgment against us.

We can only throw ourselves on God's undeserved mercy, and take from Him His freely offered gift of forgiveness of our sin, and His eternal salvation.

Undeserved!

But more wonderful than we could ever dream.

God Makes it Possible

We can't come to Jesus for His free gift of salvation and simultaneously seek to hold onto our own ways contrary to God's ways. After all, that's the very essence of sinful rebellion against the God to whom we say we're coming.

At the same time, we must not give credence to the whisper of the evil one that God's demands of us are too high, that we can't live up to His expectations. Jesus says, *Come unto me all you that labor and are heavy laden, and I will give you rest. Take my yoke upon you, and learn of me; for I am meek and lowly in heart: and you shall find rest unto your souls. For my yoke is easy, and my burden is light* (Matt. 11:28-30).

It is no burden to follow Jesus, but the most wonderful privilege in all the world, as well as the only preparation for eternity.

Moreover, He always enables us for what He asks.

Short but Sure

• Either Jesus is what He claims, the perfect Son of God, the Savior of all who believe on Him, the Determiner of destinies, or He is a fool, a liar, or self-deceived.

Which? Your answer won't change the truth, but it may determine where you will spend eternity.

• "He came to pay a debt He didn't owe, because we owed a debt we couldn't pay."

• Some people believe quite sincerely that it doesn't make much difference what god you believe in.

Suppose I believe quite sincerely that a certain medication is good for me, when in fact it will kill me? I will no less surely die when I take it.

It isn't faith that matters, or religion, but the truth.

Jesus said, *I am the way, the truth, and the life. No man comes to the Father but by me* (John 14:6).

Any other way, any other supposed truth, will not give you life, but death eternal.

• Being sure that you are saved, born again, a child of God, on your way to heaven is not a matter of feelings but of faith. God said it. I believe it. That settles it.

Still, new life and heaven are made possible by God's work alone: Jesus' death for me, His Spirit convicting me of sin, the Father forgiving me, making me His child, giving me eternal life in heaven and His own righteousness.

• For the Christian, physical death is only a promotion to eternal glory. Oh, glorious day!

To me to live is Christ, and to die is gain. . . . To be with Christ is far better. Absent from the body, and present with the Lord (Philippians 1:23; II Corinthians 5:8). Are you ready?

• Oh, what joy to be a child of the King and look forward to eternal bliss with Him forever and ever . . .

and in the meantime to walk and to talk with the King.

• God offers us peace that passes understanding. *In everything by prayer and supplication with thanksgiving, let your requests be made known unto God. And the peace of God which passes all understanding shall keep your hearts and minds through Christ Jesus* (Philippians 4:6,7).

• Senator Mark O. Hatfield once said, "I saw that for 31 years I had lived for self and decided I wanted to live the rest of my life only for Jesus Christ. I asked God to forgive my self-centered life and to make my life His own. Following Jesus Christ has been an experience of increasing challenge, adventure and happiness. Living a committed Christian life is truly satisfying because it has given me purpose and direction by serving not myself, but Jesus Christ."

Part Three—
Stories of Changed Lives

The Good Man Who Almost Missed Heaven

Harry Saulnier was brought up in church. But neither from his intensely religious parents nor from his church did he ever hear the way of salvation in Christ alone, nor the necessity of being born again to get into heaven.

When old enough, he always studied his Sunday School lesson. Even at the age of 5, he asked his teacher, "Who is Jesus?"

She replied, "We'll talk about it next Sunday." But she never did answer the boy's question.

As a young adult, while he was the center of his own apparently well-ordered world, Harry found his mind filled with questions to which he had no answer. He could not ignore the gnawing emptiness he felt within.

Finally, a coworker asked him what he did on weekends, opening the door to conversation about church. Years later this coworker, Vic Cory, founded the Christian publishing organization, Scripture

Press. At this time, he was part of North Shore Church's Fisherman's Club.

Soon Harry was hearing startling ideas like this: "Anybody would call the derelicts on Skid Row lost souls, but the most upright man in Chicago, if he's never been born again, is just as lost as one of those derelicts. The Bible says, *There is no difference, for all have sinned and come short of the glory of God.*"

Then a preacher from New York City began meetings in this church, and Harry attended. For the first time he heard the simple gospel of salvation through faith in Christ alone. But no invitation was given for the listeners to openly acknowledge that they wanted to receive Him as their Savior and Lord. Harry left the service, his heart troubled, hoping someone would offer to help him find Christ. No one did.

Finally, at home alone, he dropped to his knees, and the best he could, called on the Lord. At about 5 a.m. he wakened still on his knees, disappointed that he felt no different. At lunch time, he took out his

New Testament and read in the Gospel of John. Harry soon realized that it had taken on new life.

The next day Vic Cory invited him to the next Fisherman's Club meeting. There a man asked him, "Do you know the Lord, Brother?"

"Yes," Harry replied. And with that quick, sure affirmation, the assurance of his salvation flooded his heart.

Harry Saulnier went on to become a household name in Christian homes as Superintendent of Chicago's Pacific Garden Mission, and Director of the widely distributed radio program, *Unshackled*. His supreme goal was always to lead people, whether "down and out," or, "up and out," to Christ. And he taught the eighty-some workers under him to hold it supreme, too.

So, the most respectable of religious men almost missed heaven. And so the good man who no one would show the way to Christ was instrumental in pointing many hundreds of derelicts and others to Christ.

The Merchant Prince

John Wanamaker began his business career at 14 as an errand boy. He became the foremost businessman of Philadelphia, sometimes known as the merchant prince. He also began and superintended a Sunday School.

But he hadn't always been "religious."

Once a salesman invited him to a church meeting.

There, a handsome elderly man told how he was just waiting for God to take him home to heaven. God had given him a good life that was summed up in the statement that Christianity was a good thing to die by. Wannamaker's foolish response was that he had nothing in common with the old man.

Then, a young man said that he had just begun the Christian life. He'd been converted for two years. He said that until that time he'd had the idea that a Christian couldn't do anything that would make him happy. But he found out different. When he received Christ, a great load rolled off his heart. He became a better businessman, better able to give himself freely to his work.

Wanamaker's inward response was that he wanted to be a businessman, and here was a businessman testifying that Christianity is good to live by. The old man was testifying that Christianity is good to die by. Wanamaker said to himself that, if he were in court, and heard statements like these, he would believe them. He asked himself why—if Christianity was a good thing to live by and equally good to die by—why he didn't accept Christ right away.

So he did. He stayed until everyone left the church. Then he told the minister that he had given his heart to Jesus. The minister replied that he'd never regret it.

Wanamaker hadn't waited to get some feeling; He'd accepted the fact that he was a sinner, and Jesus was a Savior for sinners. He came to Him simply on the proposition that the gift of God is eternal life. Just like that he was Christ's, and on his way to heaven.

Dad Was Changed

My father was carried to church as a baby. Church had been central to his family for generations. He was a good boy. Then at seventeen, he goofed. The good church folk promptly turned their backs on him, and he decided he was done with church for life!

But, even in his rebellion, God hadn't forgotten him.

During the Great Depression, he moved from his family's home district. And there, in the new area, God had a man waiting for my father, a man who had been brought up in a religious home also and turned his back on it. God hadn't forsaken him either.

Several years before he met my dad, this man had turned to Christ and "got saved." And he'd never let Dad forget it. Every time they met, he'd place a loving arm around Dad, and say, "Wray, you need to get saved," or, "Wray, you need Jesus."

It was the tender heartedness, the caring, shown by Craig Harris, that got to my dad.

One day he was traveling a

distance of about 30 miles. The entire way he talked to God. He asked the Lord again and again to save him. But nothing happened. As he drew near his destination, he asked God, "What do I have to I do to be saved?"

Now, knowing my dad, he was probably frustrated, perhaps a little angry with God. But that didn't concern God greatly. As, later, he loved to tell the story over and over, he'd say, "Almost as clearly as though it were aloud, I heard God say to me, 'It's not do. It's done.'"

And from that day to his death at 83 years, he was delightedly clear that there wasn't a thing he could do to earn salvation. He knew that when Jesus said in dying on the cross, *It is finished*, He had done absolutely everything necessary for the eternal salvation of every human being who will believe and receive Him as his or her personal Savior.

If you trust in anyone or anything other than Christ and His finished work on the cross for your salvation, you are eternally lost. If you trust in Christ and His finished work on the cross alone for your salvation, you are saved eternally. Dad loved this truth.

By grace are you saved through faith, and that not of yourselves, it is the gift of God, not of works, lest any man should boast (Ephesians 2:8,9).

Two other scripture passages were also especially dear to Him. *The heart is deceitful above all things, and desperately wicked: who can know it?* (Jeremiah 17:9). *If any man be in Christ, he is a new creature: old things are passed away; behold, all things are become new* (II Corinthians 5:17).

When he received Christ as his Savior, he took Him also as Lord of his life, and the differences were immediate. Every noon hour he studyied his Bible and prayed.

He hadn't been a drunk because he "could hold his liquor." But, it had bothered him greatly for a long time that he had money for liquor and tobacco but not to put butter on his children's bread!

Being Scottish, he always liked

the smell of "good whiskey." But as he would tell it, "God delivered me from alcohol immediately. I never touched another drop."

Soon, as he was driving along, he saw an old man tilling the land and smoking. He was revolted by the scene and of it said afterward. "Suddenly there was a sting in my mouth like that caused by a dirty pipe. I threw away my tobacco and never wanted it again."

But he knew well the deceitfulness of his heart, and despised it. His quick temper plagued him until the end of his life on earth, though increasingly tempered by a kind and caring spirit.

Nothing ever delighted Dad more than to be part of leading people to Christ. Soon after he received Jesus, he helped start a home meeting where he played the violin, and one of my sisters played the piano. There I learned the scriptures that he and other new Christians loved to quote, and at six years I would ask questions and make comments. These home meetings became a mission in Elora,

Ontario, Canada.

They grew into the Bethel Baptist church of nearby Fergus. Dad was the only paid worker on the initial building project, as those interested literally tore down an abandoned church building brick by brick and moved it some 20 miles. From that church, the good news of salvation in Christ has gone out around the world. And I can hear Dad now saying, "Let God get the praise."

A Changed Life, Great Suffering, A Changed Nation

Just as William Carey was the father of the British missionary enterprise, so Adoniram Judson was of the American.

Judson was brilliant, reading at 3, taking navigation lessons at 10.

Though his father was a minister, and despite his mother's prayers, as a teen, he became an atheist. Then one night in a country inn, Judson heard the moans and groans of the man who lay dying in the next room. All night questions assailed his soul: "Was the dying man prepared to die? Where would he spend eternity?"

The next morning he discovered that the man who died there was the young man who had led him into atheism. Now he was dead and lost. This word plagued his mind and soul, "Lost! Lost! Lost!"

Judson knew he was lost too, and seeking help, found Christ as Savior.

His conversion not only saved his soul, it smashed his dreams of fame and honor for himself. His one pressing purpose became to "plan his life to please his Lord," and he started preparing to go to the mission field.

With his bride he sailed for India. But, on arrival, he was not allowed entry. After terrible difficulties, they went to Burma. They found not one Christian among its millions, and no friends, but constant danger to their lives. A new baby died soon after their arrival.

For six years there was not a single convert, but he said, "I will not leave Burma until the cross is planted here forever."

He was imprisoned for 17 months as a spy: suffered horribly, nearly starved, in heat and cold, suspended at night by ropes, his head lower than his feet. Though his wife scarcely had food enough for herself and their little girl, she constantly smuggled food and writing materials in to him. There he translated much of the Bible into Burmese.

Then their little girl died.

Judson translated the whole Bible into Burmese and created a dictionary. He returned only once briefly to America.

In 1850, thirty years after Adoniram Judson's death, Burma had 63 Christian churches, 163 missionaries, and over 7000 baptized believers.

Part Four—
More Stories,
Etc.

Have A Good Day, Friend

I wish we could sit down together and talk . . . that we could rip off our masks and share as friends . . . that I could tell you that, though I can be terribly selfish, I really do care what happens to you.

I'd like to show you I'm not alone in caring. There are millions of others who care too and who will be sharing their caring today.

These caring people are rich, poor, educated, illiterate, black, white, oriental, Protestant, Catholic, African, European, American, Canadian, but they care because they're God's people.

They weren't born that way. In fact, they'll tell you they were born separated— estranged—from God.

They aren't good. They'll tell you "there is none good."

They aren't even really religious. They have something that makes mere religion insignificant.

They're trusting people . . . trusting God's mercy to meet their need.

And He has.

They were lonely, and He came to

be with them always.

They were frightened, and He gave them His peace.

They felt hopeless, and He gave them hope.

They worried about living . . . and even more about dying . . . and He took away their fear.

He can do the same for you—if you'll just ask Him to.

Turn to page 53.

If you haven't yet received Christ as your Lord and Savior, pray the Prayer of Faith now.

Mean it from your heart.

Then continue your reading from there with a heart full of gratitude to God for making you His own, forgiving you, cleansing you, making you new, and giving you eternal life and an eternal home in heaven.

Request copies of this piece in leaflet form. See how at back.

How Much Time Do You Have?

We were married for 45 years. Of these, for 32 years, my beautiful Ruthie had Parkinson's Disease.

After 25 of these, we wrote the story I'll repeat in just a minute. Probably 30,000 copies have been distributed at the time of this writing.

I remember so well giving one of these leaflets to a waitress in Virginia. When we returned to the same restaurant the next day, I discovered that our waitress was the owner of the place. She told us she had called all her staff together before they went home and she had read Ruthie's little story to them. Every one of them had teary eyes as they listened.

Ruthie loved nothing more than to have a part in pointing people to Jesus. And when the Lord took her Home to be with Him, He arranged for the Buffalo News to run a headline acknowledging, "Ruth V. Marr, Promoted Evangelism." I'm sure it delighted her in heaven.

Now, here is that little story. I'm sure she's happy it's included in this book and you're reading it—

When you look at the clock, does it ever strike you that your time is very short on this earth?

I'm desperately aware of it!

You see, I've had Parkinson's Disease for over 25 years. I take medication and special nutrients costing up to $200 a week, and thank the Lord, they've kept me alive. But the effectiveness of the medication wears off, and, as I take more and more, the side effects get worse and worse. I'm in agony. The pain in my ribs and waist is unbearable.

I often can't stop wiggling because the medication has damaged nerve ends in the brain. This constant movement produces pain somewhere in my body most of the time unless I'm massaged frequently.

When I'm immobilized, my brain doesn't get enough oxygen, and the emotional stress is sometimes more than I can cope with! Hallucinations have become nearly constant.

There are still many things I'd like to do, places I'd like to go. I'd like to see the old farm where I was born once more. I'd like to see my brothers and sisters again. I'd like to enjoy another merry-go-round ride. But these things aren't important.

Eternal life is.

I can't possibly tell you how glad I am that death holds no great fear for me. I'm so glad I'm sure of where I'm going to spend eternity. And I'd like everyone else to be sure, too.

If you know Jesus, it's important that you go across the street and tell that neighbor Jesus loves him and died on the cross so he can have his sins forgiven and life eternal.

Maybe he never heard, and if you don't tell him, no one will, and he'll spend eternity in hell instead of heaven.

I'm naturally shy and the disease makes it hard for me to write or talk. So, how can I tell those I care for about Jesus?

Perhaps this little piece of paper will serve the purpose. It tells you that you're lost if you've never accepted my Friend, Jesus. It tells you that you need more than anything else in the world to receive Him as your Savior right now. Only then can you be sure of heaven.

-Ruthie Peters Marr

Request copies of this story in leaflet form. See how at the back of this book.

Better Than We Dream

Loyd had been seriously ill for nearly a year. His family, and especially his wife, Gladys, hurt with his hurt. They'd been married 61 years, and were very close. He had become less and less able to walk, talk, or think until at last, bed bound entirely, he seemed unable even to recognize her.

I had no idea that the end was near, so the call telling me he'd "passed on" took me by surprise. My immediate reaction was to pray for Gladys and the family. And my prayer was this, "Lord, don't let them feel guilty that they're glad He's gone, released from all his sufferings, at home with you."

Before the memorial service, as I hugged Gladys, my mind was quickly set at ease. Her face was radiant, and her first words were, "It's an answer to prayer."

Then she talked about the thunderstorm the previous night, calling it "fireworks that welcomed Loyd Home."

Now, it isn't strange that people in such a circumstance should feel relieved both for themselves and for the one whose physical pain here on earth is finally done.

But there was an entirely different factor in this story. Loyd was far better off than he had ever been, far better off than all those he had left behind. He was finally at Home in heaven with his loving heavenly Father and his wonderful Savior. He was perfectly healthy as he never had been before. In fact, he was perfectly everything. And, oh, how he had longed for such perfection all the days of his imperfection down here.

There was something more. Gladys and the rest of them had no need to feel guilty. They looked forward to that glad reunion day, when they would all be with Loyd in a perfect relationship far better than they could ever enjoy here.

Now, this isn't necessarily your final future. The next story tells a completely different tale. Which will it be for you?

Have you prayed the Prayer of Faith? If not, don't delay. Your day to leave this life and enter on the next may be closer than you imagine. You dare not risk postponing the most important decision of your life for a single moment.

Turn to page 53 now. Pray the Prayer of Faith. You'll be glad forever you did.

Request copies of this story in leaflet form. See how at back.

Jesus' Story of Hell

A certain rich man, who was clothed in purple and fine linen, fared sumptuously every day.

And there was a certain beggar, named Lazarus, who was laid at his gate, full of sores, and desiring to be fed from the crumbs which fell from the rich man's table; moreover, the dogs came and licked his sores.

And it came to pass that the beggar died, and was carried by the angels into Abraham's bosom; the rich man also died and was buried; and in hell he lifted up his eyes, being in torments, and saw Abraham afar off, and Lazarus in his bosom.

He cried, saying, Father Abraham have mercy on me, and send Lazarus that he may dip the tip of his finger

98

in water, and cool my tongue; for I am tormented in this flame.

But Abraham said, Son, remember that you in your lifetime received your good things, and likewise Lazarus evil things; but now he is comforted, and you are tormented.

And beside all this, between us and you there is a great gulf fixed, so that they who would pass from here to you cannot; neither can they pass to us that would come from there.

Then he said, I pray you, therefore, father, that you would send him to my father's house. (For I have five brothers), that he may testify unto them, lest they also come into this place of torment.

Abraham said unto him, They have Moses and the prophets; let them hear them.

And he said, No, father Abraham; but if one went unto them from the dead, they will repent.

And he said unto him, If they hear not Moses and the prophets, neither will they be persuaded, though one rose from the dead (Luke 6:19-31).

The Price of Love

There was once a big turntable bridge spanning a large river.

Most of the time, the bridge sat with its length running parallel to the river so ships could pass freely on both sides of it.

Whenever a train was expected, the bridge was turned to cross the river, then locked securely in position to allow the train safe passage.

A switchman sat in a little shack on one side of the river. From there he could operate the controls.

One evening the switchman turned to the controls to allow the last train of the day to cross. He got the bridge into position without difficulty. But, to his horror, the locking mechanism wouldn't work. Unless the tracks locked securely, the train would surely jump the track and go crashing into the river with its cargo of human passengers. For such an emergency there was a manual locking lever on the far side of the river.

Knowing there was no time to waste, he hurried to it. But to get it to work, he had to hold the lever firmly in position as the train roared on.

Then he heard a sound that made his blood run cold: "Daddy, where are you?"

His four-year-old son was crossing the bridge to look for him.

The father's first impulse was to call to the child, "Run! Run!" But the train was too close, the tiny legs would never get the child across the bridge in time.

Oh, how he wanted to let go the lever, snatch the child into his arms and carry him to safety. But he'd never make it back to the lever on time. Either the people in the train or his little son must die.

His heart breaking, he held the lever in position until the train passed safely.

No one aboard was aware of the tiny, broken body thrown mercilessly into the river by the rushing train. Nor were they aware of the pitiful figure of the sobbing man still clinging tightly to the lever. They didn't see the grief-stricken father dragging himself home to tell his wife he had sacrificed their son to save the train load of passengers he didn't even know.

Now, imagine what our loving heavenly Father must have felt when He sacrificed His perfect Son to save even those who reject Him and His love?

Love indeed.

Love beyond comprehension.

Can you be so wickedly ungrateful as to continue rejecting Him who has done so much for you?

To do so is to invite the eternal displeasure of the Almighty God who longs to be your loving Father.

Behold, what manner of love the Father has bestowed on us. . . . In this was manifested the love of God toward us, because that God sent his only begotten Son into the world, that we might live through him. Herein is love, not that we loved God, but that He loved us, and sent his Son to be the propitiation (sacrifice) for our sins. . . . We love him because he first loved us (I John 3:1; 4:9-11,19).

He Loved You So Much!

Jesus died what might be the most excruciatingly painful death ever endured by a man. A crown of thorns was crushed into His head, blood running into his eyes, nose, and mouth, blinding and choking Him. Nails were driven through His hands and feet. As the cross was dropped cruelly into its socket in the ground, His flesh tore with searing pain. A spear pierced His side. Blood emptied from every wound until each cell in His body screamed for water and nourishment.

But, incredible as it may seem, He endured still greater pain than this.

Remember, though fully man, He was also perfect God. He could not endure to look on sin with any semblance of approval. Now, He actually *bore our sin in His own body on the tree. He became sin for us.*

All mankind's awful sins were placed on Jesus' perfect person so that Father God had to turn His back on Jesus the Son, through no fault of either of them.

From eternity past the Son had always been in perfect loving harmony with God the Father.

Now, He had to cry out in awful distress, *My God, my God, why have you forsaken me?* (Mark 15:34).

We can't begin to fathom the terrible agony that all this entailed for both of them.

Jesus experienced immeasurable moral imperfection replacing the absolute moral perfection that had always been His from eternity. This was pain beyond imagining.

And God the Father's limitless love for Him was reduced to total rejection. This was inner pain unfathomable. Such suffering beyond understanding or expression, He suffered for you!

Do you care?

Will you keep on neglecting Him who loved you so—who keeps right on loving you?

There's a limit beyond which even His boundless love cannot go. Accept His love today.

Before it is too late.

If you haven't yet, receive Him as your Savior and Lord now.

That's right.

NOW!

Now is the only time you have.

Turn to page 53, and pray the Prayer of Faith now.

Who (Jesus) bore our sins in His own body on the tree, that we, being dead to sins, should live unto righteousness: by whose stripes you were healed (I Peter 2:24).

He has made Him who knew no sin to be sin for us, that we might be made the righteousness of God in Him (I Corinthians 5:21).

Therefore, we ought to give the more earnest heed to the things which we have heard. . . . How shall we escape if we neglect so great salvation (Hebrews 2:1,3).

Get Me Out of Here

Nurse Connie shared her love for Christ with her patients often. One man she would never forget. He mocked her faith with comments like, "I'll be ok. I'll be playing cards with my friends in hell."

But when it came to the end, he sent for Connie. When she arrived, he grabbed her and held on. He pulled on her arm until she thought he'd pull it right out of its socket.

He pled with her over and over again, "Get me out of here."

So he passed into the world he had mocked and faced the God he had shunned.

What about Connie? She asked herself over and over, "Could I have done more to try to lead this man to Christ?"

She wished she'd been able to bring him to the Savior he needed and spurned.

Don't let this man's story be yours. Don't wait a moment longer. If you haven't yet, receive Jesus as your Savior and Lord today.

The Simple Truth

Now, if I could urge you to read one part of the Bible, it would be the Gospel of John, for in it the beloved disciple tells all who will listen how to have eternal life. Near the end of this wonderful book he says, *Many other signs truly did Jesus in the presence of His disciples, which are not written in this book: but these are written, that you might believe that Jesus is the Christ, the Son of God; and that believing you might have life through His name* (John 20:30, 31).

Near the beginning of the book, John felt it necessary to clarify what he means by believing. He wants it to be so clear we can't miss it, because, after all, on that one word depends the eternal destiny of every human being. To clarify what he means by believing, John said, *"As many as received Him (Jesus), to them gave He power to become the sons of God, even to them that believe on His name."* If we truly believe in Jesus, we will receive Him as our personal Lord and Savior, asking Him to come into our hearts and lives, forgive our sins, and give us a home in heaven with Him eternally.

He cannot save everyone. He can save only those who are willing to see themselves as lost sinners worthy of eternal condemnation, those willing to cast themselves upon Him as their only hope. He cannot save those who hope somehow to be good enough to get to

107

heaven by their good deeds.

Nor can he save those whose trust is in the church, or baptism, or catechism, or any religious belief or experience. It is He alone who died for our sins on the cruel cross, sent there by love for us who didn't love Him at all.

Nor can He save any who do not believe in Him and receive Him as their Savior and Lord. He said, *I am the way, the truth, and the life, no man comes to the father but by me* (John 14:6). He is our only hope.

If you haven't yet prayed the Prayer of Faith with meaning, turn to page 53 and pray it earnestly now.

Fantastic Benefits Right Now

I've told you often what is going to follow this life—eternal life in the most perfect situation that you could ever imagine, or terrible eternal condemnation.

In the meantime, in the here and now, those of us who receive Jesus as our Savior can have His presence, His peace and His power, His wisdom, His fellowship, His comfort, and His joy.

At the same time our faith will be tested. We may suffer the pains of this life much as do those who don't know Christ as Savior. We may also be rejected by those who reject the Savior. Around the world there are always people being martyred for their faith.

On average, however, those who are Jesus' benefit in the here and now. Those who *genuinely* follow Jesus have happier families, more peace of mind, and even healthier bodies. There have been studies over the years indicating that those who go to church regularly, or those who pray often, benefit from it. God promised, *I will never leave you, nor forsake you* (Hebrews 13:5).

No matter the pain we may endure, the Lord is with us and in us, comforting us, encouraging us, guiding us, and caring for our needs. He has given us hundreds of wonderful promises.

Here are a few:

My God shall supply all your need according to His riches in glory by Christ Jesus (Philippians 4:19).

Seek first the kingdom of God, and His righteousness, and all these things (physical necessities) shall be added to you (Matthew 6:33).

All things work together for good to them that love God, to them who are the called according to His purpose (Romans 8:28).

Draw near to God, and He will draw near to you (James 4:8).

Humble yourself in the sight of the Lord, and He shall lift you up (James 4:10).

Does God Keep His Promises?

George Muller was a young reprobate brought up in a religious home in Germany. He was supposed to train to be a minister, but had no time for God. He stole to keep up his bad habits—specially from his father.

Finally, he received Jesus as his Savior, and his life was completely changed.

He moved to England and became a minister. He told the church he pastored that he didn't want a salary, but would simply receive whatever was placed in containers set for that purpose at the back of the church.

Sometimes the person appointed to empty the containers and give the contents to Mr. Muller would forget to do it. Still, Muller always had enough to meet his needs.

He started an orphanage, refusing ever to make his needs generally known, taking them, instead, to God in earnest prayer. Even when the orphanages grew until they cared for 2000 children, he still always found their needs met.

His stories of God's miraculous provision numbered in the hundreds. One morning they had no milk for breakfast. A knock came on the door. A man said, "My milk cart has broken down. The milk will spoil. Can you use it?"

God also led Hudson Taylor not to ask people for money for his Christian work. Taylor founded the great China Inland Mission. It was at a time when the quickest communication between China and England was about four months by ship. Many were the trials, but God always provided. And guess who He often used to convey that provision? None other than George Muller.

Yes, my friend, God is real. He keeps His promises. He cares for His own.

After ministering for almost fifty years, most of it without salary, after caring for my wife with Parkinson's Disease for 32 of those years until the Lord called her Home to be with Him, after many terrible trials, I too, can testify that He is always faithful.

Part Five—
WHERE WILL YOU BE 100 YEARS FROM NOW?

I'm unusual.

I look forward to dying.

Oh, yes, there's the normal tug of this life and this world.

In spite of the pain I've endured, there are good things, too. There's the beauty of the trees, the flowers, the hills and mountains, the nearby Niagara Falls. There's the beautiful birds with their sweet songs. There's family and friends. And most there's God and His love.

Perhaps it's not really the dying that I look forward to.

It's what comes next.

The unpleasantness of dying is just the prelude to a perfect eternity for me.

And that's the rub.

I Can't Stand the Present Imperfections

I don't like the imperfections of this world. Even the most wonderful things this world offers are flawed by imperfections of all kinds, and they're fleeting at best.

When I go to nearby Lake Ontario, and gaze, and enjoy, and relish the tranquility I feel, I can't stand the idea that I can't take it all away with me.

Just so, I hate the certainty that the beauty of the new warm green of spring and the magnificent multicolors of fall will be followed by the cold gray-brown bareness of winter.

I can't stand the hurtful imperfections that are the common lot of all mankind. I loathe my own worst of all.

I long for the day when I will at last escape from all the uncertainties, failures, follies, stupidities, and imperfections of all kinds that are so obviously mine.

Is There Really Life After Death?

"But," you ask, "what makes you think you're going to live on in any form after you die?"

Well, in the first place I'm not really going to die at all. Never. My body may die, be buried, and return dust to dust. But my soul, the real me will live on.

Now, the question isn't so much whether we're going to live on after death.

Is There a God?

The real question is, "Is there a personal, all-powerful, all-knowing, everywhere-present, eternal, and infinite God who created all that is?"

Any other answer than, "Yes, obviously He is," is quite ridiculous.

Look up at the stars. Look out at the world. Look in at your body, and most notably at your brain. There can be no other answer.

Billions of brain cells work together to accomplish the most marvelous feats. Every organ plays its role in the human body. If it weren't there, or if it weren't designed to work exactly as it does work, the body wouldn't function. When almost any organ stops functioning, the whole stops functioning, and you die.

There are billions of stars in our galaxy and billions of such galaxies in our universe. Suspended in space, they operate in the most awe-inspiring order.

The earth's ecosystem is so marvelously balanced that, from tigers to microbes, vultures to rabbits, it functions to keep every-thing in it operating effectively. Every creature is provided with all it needs to operate adequately in its environment.

Now, go ahead, tell me that all this came about by unplanned accident. Tell me there is no God. And hear God reply from His book, the Bible, *"The fool has said in his heart, there is no God"* (Psalm 14:1).

A noted biologist, the late professor Edwin Conklin, declared the probability of life originating by accident is comparable to the probability of the Unabridged Dictionary resulting from an explosion in a printing shop.

George Gallup, the statistician, said: "I could prove God statistically. Take the human body alone . . . the chance that all the functions of the individual would just happen is a statistical monstrosity."

The Devil's Awful Lies

The devil says there's no God, no life after death, no eternally perfect place prepared for God's then-perfected children, no everlasting punishment.

A long time ago this same devil told another lie. He told Eve, the mother of the race, "You shall not surely die." When he told that lie, he introduced into the earth and the human race not only death, but all the anguish, hurt, pain, and suffering; all the uncertainty, the frustration, the loneliness; and all the sin and evil that have cursed mankind ever since. Satan works to take men with him into the hell God provided for the devil and his angels.

God Provided a Way Out.

But the God who created mankind loved you too much. He wanted no part in this. He arranged for an end to all the pain, suffering, sin and hell for all of those who would accept His way out.

He sent Jesus, His sinless Son, to die on the cross, taking our sin and punishment on Himself. And His Spirit is pursuing you relentlessly, calling you to turn from your sin and receive Him as your Savior and Lord.

You Don't Believe—So What?

Now, you don't have to believe any of this. You don't have to take Him as your Savior. No one can force you.

The choice is yours. But it's a none-choice. Do you really want to choose the devil's way, not God's? Do you really want to choose your sin, not your Savior? Do you really want to choose hell, not heaven?

"But," you say, "I don't believe there's a heaven or hell."

My dear friend, that doesn't make a bit of difference. A minute after you're dead you'll be a believer. Then, it will be too late.

So, to seek God and His salvation must be right now the very most important concern of your life. Turn to page 53. Pray the Prayer of Faith with meaning. If you haven't yet, receive Christ now as your personal Savior and your Lord.

Part Six—
A SUMMARY

I really do care for you. And I'd like to show it by asking you to answer the five most important questions you'll ever be asked.

HERE THEY ARE . . .

—Do you believe Jesus Christ died for our sins on the cross, was buried, and rose from the dead after three days?
(I Corinthians 15:3,4)

☐ YES ☐ NO

—Do you admit you are a sinner? (Do you do things God does not like?)
(Romans 3:23)

☐ YES ☐ NO

—Do you agree to turn from sin to God? (Are you willing to turn away from things God does not like as best as you know how right now?)
(Acts 20:24)

☐ YES ☐ NO

—Do you acknowledge Jesus is Lord? (Are you willing to recognize Jesus as God with a right to direct your life?) (Romans 10:9)

☐YES ☐NO

—Do you accept God's free gift of salvation? (It is a free gift, no strings attached. You cannot earn it.) (Ephesians 2:8)

☐YES ☐NO

—Now, will you pray the Prayer of Faith? (See page 53.)

Signed:_____

Being Sure You Have Eternal Life

If you have responded to God's call, honestly and sincerely said "yes" to those five questions, prayed the Prayer of Faith, and meant it in your heart, then you may have the assurance of eternal life.

If you will confess with your mouth the Lord Jesus, and believe in your heart that God has raised Him from the dead, you will be saved. For with the heart man believes unto righteousness, and with the mouth confession is made unto salvation (Romans 10:9,10).

This is the record that God has given us eternal life, and this life is in His Son. He that has the Son has life; and he that has not the Son of God has not life. These things have I written unto you that believe on the name of the Son of God, that you may know that you have eternal life (I John 5:11-13).

If You Said No . . .

If you had to answer "No" to any of these questions, let me thank you for your honesty.

Now, if I could get you information that would help you say "Yes" to that question, would you read it?"

Let me know you'd like it, so I can do my best to get it for you.

See how at the back of this book.

What Next?

If you have answered "Yes" to all these questions, prayed the Prayer of Faith, and received Jesus as your personal Savior and Lord, what do you do next?

•First and foremost, be sure you tell someone you've received Jesus Christ as your Lord and Savior. Why not tell the friend who gave you this book, or the author? See addresses and phone numbers at back.

•Read your Bible frequently to discover God's message for you (II Timothy 3:15-17). Begin with the Gospel of John.

124

•Talk to God in prayer often about yourself and others. (Philippians 4:6,7)

•By God's enabling, develop a lifestyle consistent with Bible principles. (I John 2:6)

•Tell others about Christ in your own way. (Acts 1:8) Why not write me for copies of gospel tracts to distribute.

•Faithfully attend a Bible-teaching church for worship and fellowship. (Hebrews 10:24,25).

•Set a time aside daily to fellowship with God in worship, thanksgiving, praise, adoration, listening, and quiet waiting on Him.

•Read and study good devotional books to encourage you in your walk with the Lord.

I will be glad to send you a list upon request and a copy of my book, *A Christianity That Really Works*, as God may enable. See our postal, e-mail, and web addresses, and phone number at back.

Once you're sure of your own salvation, eternal life, and home in heaven, you should ask these five questions often of friends and acquaintances, and so lead them also to know Christ as their Savior. This is the most important task of every Christian.

If we have the love of God in our hearts, we will not be satisfied until we've done our best by the Holy Spirit's enabling to try to bring all our friends and acquaintances to Christ.

Ron Marr is author also of these books, *A Christianity That Really Works* and *Spiritual Dynamite* (Whitaker House Publishers), and hundreds of articles.

For more information on how you can be sure of heaven, and on how to get copies of this book and other Christian literature contact:

ChristLife, Inc.
1642 Michigan Avenue
Niagara Falls, NY 14305
Tel: 716-284-7625
Fax: 716-285-5409
E-Mail: pastormarr@adelphia.net
christlife@adelphia.net
Web Sites: www.pastormarr.com
www.christpassion.net

Help get this message out as widely as possible at home and around the world. Who knows how many lives and destinies you may help change? A private printing or even a private edition may be arranged for organizations or churches.

At publishing date ChristLife's Suggested Minimum Donation per copy of this book was for 100 copies $200, 50 copies $125, 20 copies $60, 10 copies $35, 1 to 9 copies $4 each.

This book is given with care by

_____